Thoughtful Teenager

Dr. Ekhoriyayi Lilian Arigidi

Thoughtful Teenager

Dr. Ekhoriyayi Lilian Arigidi

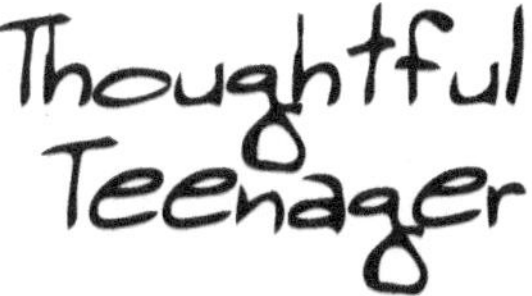

Published in Nigeria by
Parousia Publishing
(An Alakowe Firm)

Address: Rufai Olayiwola Complex, Benjamin Bus Stop, Eleyele, Ibadan, Oyo State, Nigeria.

Phone No: +2347030874764, +15642245556
Email: info@parousiacollective.com, parousiareads@gmail.com
Website: www.parousiamag.com
          www.parousiacollective.com

PAROUSIA

TABLE OF CONTENTS

INTRODUCTION

What are you aiming towards?

To live a life of purpose is to be intentional and thoughtful about something.

Teenagers' lives are ever-changing, and they live in a society with swift innovations and varied information at their fingertips. It can be tough to figure out what to do next when juggling homework, extracurricular activities, and social life.

Lack of purpose is not just an adult's problem. It hits young people as well. Suicide is currently the third leading cause of death for our teenagers; they see no point in living, and nothing makes sense. The younger generation are both curious and concerned about their future.

Only a few of them feel well-prepared for adulthood.

This book equips you with fundamental truths to be thoughtful about in order to explore gracefully and become whom God wants you to be.

The existence of anything was thought of to be what it is, and as a teenager, your existence at this stage was carefully thought of by God.

Chapter 1

AS A TEENAGER

'Remember now your Creator in the days of your youth, before the evil days come and the years draw near when you say, I have no pleasure in them' (Eccl. 12:1)

Eccl. 7:20 also tells us there is none a person that is perfect on earth who always does well.

Understanding who you are and accepting your person as a teenager defines you. It takes a thoughtful teenager to know this. When you are thoughtful in all things, you will be mindful in all you do. The thought of yourself and what you perceive from others affect your outlook/image, either positive or negative. For instance, if you do not have a positive impression of yourself, you might begin to push yourself until you start to perceive yourself as perfect or imperfect.

A better you stems from first knowing who you are, then accepting that person, and adding value to yourself.

Timing for every teenager, in terms of physical development, will be discussed in this series, while nature, nurture and mindset will be addressed in the next. One of a teenager's experiences is the gradual physical developmental changes. The remarkable transformation is that which takes place in your brain and is absolutely normal. Questions like, "What is happening to me?" "Am I okay?" "Why am I so big?" "Why is my hair scanty?" and so on keep popping into your head as a result of these transformations. If not controlled, this could lead to aggravations, ebullience, insecurities, pressures and risk-taking.

The timing of physical and developmental changes varies throughout adolescence: yours could come early or late; either way, development does not imply high or low body image that may sometimes translate to a wrong perception of yourself. Invariably, the change you see happening to others or what they say about you should not define who you are as a teenager.

My point is that understanding these changes, whether early or late, helps you to appreciate first who you are as a teenager and who you are in Christ. A teenager who understands his or her developmental transformation is focused, irrespective of the changes being experienced. Mind you, this comes with responsibilities that will speak a lot about your character. Understanding the process of your developmental changes brings about a healthy perception of self which will help you sift through the bombard of negative messages related to your body image, beauty standards, appearance, attractiveness and rejections that you encounter in the media, at home, and from friends.

This period is a positive transition for you to be equipped to fulfil your plan and purpose in life. God says, *"For the plan I have for you are plans to prosper you and not to harm you, plans to give you hope and a future" (Jeremiah 29:11)*. Only those who are ready and have positively transformed can fit into the plan of God for their lives. A good tree cannot bear good fruits if its seed had not first been buried in the soil and then subjected to rain and sunshine to grow and transform from a tender plant into a tree bearing good fruits.

For me, growing up as a teenager was quite a smooth sail to the glory of God. This was because I was privileged to be taught of the Lord by my father, who was my first teacher. He bombarded me with almost everything I needed to know like it is my life. I used to feel he was not giving me breathing space back then, but today, I am glad because it guided me through the valley of the shadow of this world.

Once you understand who you are, you must be:

1. Obedient to God

Obedience is from a Latin word meaning "to hear." It is connected to trust and respect. When we obey God, it is a sign that we trust Him and are listening to what He is saying, and truly believe He knows best. If we don't obey God, we are essentially saying, "I know better than You do," which was precisely what happened in the Garden of Eden. Adam and Eve, our first parents, rejected God's authority and fell into sin. After the fall, the original state of perfect communion between God and man was broken, meaning we can no longer know what God wants for us without being told.

Only God knows what is best for us and our happiness. When we try to do things our way, we make mistakes and fall short of the goal. Obeying God is the only way to know we are doing the right thing, which will work out for the best for everyone, including ourselves, in the end. Even if we don't immediately understand all of God's commands, we must trust in His Wisdom and obey.

Our modern culture really pushes freedom to the point of contradicting ourselves. We have been subtly and not so subtly told that as long as we accept anyone's authority over us, we are not really free. Our fallen nature is constantly in rebellion against God and falls under the control of temptations, worldly cultural influences, and selfish desires—this form of "freedom" is the greatest slavery of all.

In the book of Romans, the Bible teaches us that you are a slave to the one you obey, whether to righteousness or to sin. Romans 9:32 says that we obey the law by faith, not as though it were by works. Romans 14:23 says, *"Whatever does not proceed from faith is sin,"* which means any attempt at obedience, or any other act that isn't springing from a heart of faith, winds up just being a sin because it displeases the Lord.

"Without faith, it is impossible to please God"
Hebrews 11:6

God created you to live for him (Colossians 1:16). You'll only be happy if you do so. Don't give in to peer pressure. Peer pressure often leads you to sin in some way- for instance, when you want to have it your way, overeating, drinking alcohol, having premarital sex, covetousness, lying to excuse yourself, etc.

Please don't give in... It's not worth it!

- **Obedient to your parent**

Our parents deserve the highest of regard from us in the world. If you think you have no reason at all, reflect on the fact that you could only see the light of the world through them. We were practically in a helpless condition when you and I were born. We could not have survived if they had not cared for us in our infancy. They watched over us when we were ill and always do their best to make us good and happy.

Parents are delighted if their son or daughter is kind, polite, helpful, and obedient. It is disappointing and hurts a parent when the case is otherwise. After all, the way a teen behaves reflects on his parents.

At each point, be thoughtful enough to understand that your decisions are not all about you alone, it also affects your parent.

Every teenager must obey and honour their parents in order to live a fruitful life. (Ephesians 6:1-4)

I know you probably think your parents are uncool and they sometimes get on your nerves (believe me, you get on their nerves too), but God ordained them that they (oh yes! your mother and your father) would be your parents, and He commands that you obey them. While you may sometimes disagree with your parents, the truth is you will always regret it when you disobey them.

Obey your mother and father because it pays to do so. Learn to listen and obey first, then find the appropriate time to express your opinion clearly in humility.

That, my dear, is wisdom.

- **Obedient to authorities**

Paul says, *"Let every person be subject to the governing authorities" (Romans 13:1).* Paul then calls the authorities' God's servants' and 'ministers of God' (v .4, v.6). In Greek, the words that Paul used for these two verses are the exact words he used when speaking about Christian ministers of the church elsewhere.

Here's the point: God wants you to respect and obey authorities.

At your age, it may seem cool to be rebellious to authority. But that is one of the biggest problems with your generation and mine: lack of respect for authority. Whether your teacher, principal, pastor or grandparent, you must understand that certain people have authority over you to protect you, and you owe them that respect. Don't ever think you have grown physically to know everything. You are still growing into who God wants you to be.

As teenagers, there are certain things that we can learn - not only about how to fulfil our own roles, but also how we can make the other person's role easier for him to fulfil. We should remember that how we fulfil our obligations toward others will often have a strong influence on how they fulfil their own obligations toward us. And even when it doesn't help and the situation remains bad, it will not be our fault.

Remember that the day is coming in which each of us will give account to the final Judge who is over all, and it will be for our own actions and responses, not for another's.

Both the people in positions of authority as well as those who are in submission all have tendencies to do things in ways contrary to the scriptures. The problem is not the authority structures themselves but the willingness to obey, knowing that it will bring good results.

Romans 13:1 - Everyone must obey/submit to the governing authorities. They have been put there by God.

In Acts 12:13, when Peter knocked at the outer door, a servant girl named Rhoda came to answer the door [i.e., to "obey" the knocking for the door to be opened]. She was so overjoyed when she saw Peter that she momentarily forgot to "obey" the knocking! This verse describes a servant girl who was simply doing her job as a servant. However, maybe it would be a good time for us to reflect on our willingness to do what we know we should be doing.

Sometimes unexpected blessings occur as we do what we know we're supposed to do! You do not need to pursue this type of blessing. God gives it without warning; we only need to be willing to see and not be ignorant and blind about how God works in our lives.

- **Be diligent.**

As a preteen at twelve, Jesus already knew who He was. He focused on doing his Father's business and taking responsibility. Luke 2:49.

The inspiration behind this book is to create an early awakening in your spirit and cause you to be thoughtful about everything, taking full responsibility for your action in every day-to-day activity.

As Proverbs 22:29 tells us, *'seest thou a man diligent in his business? He shall stand before kings; he shall not stand before mean men.'*

You may ask, but I don't have a business.

Yes, your business now is your academics and service to God. You must be diligent about it in order to be on top and above your peers. Diligence is one of the traits that most teenagers find hard to achieve. With the increasing number of distractions around, such as social media, the internet, and mobile games, it becomes difficult to stay focused on what needs to be done.

Admit it: once you feel tired or bored with what you do, you tend to leave it for the meantime and go somewhere else to enjoy yourself.

However, being diligent or hard-working should be one of your top qualities if you want to be successful. It allows you to accomplish more in lesser time without sacrificing quality. A diligent teenager sees the possibilities of a great future and understands it will take a lot of hard work and determination to see it through to reality. On the contrary, the lazy person does not see the possibility of anything good happening; he rather sees problems, and everyone but himself is always at fault because he never wants to take the responsibility to be diligent.

A thoughtful teenager wanting to see changes in his life asks questions about what to do to make things different instead of idly wishing for something good to happen. Even when you are in the waiting season of your life, keep at something and be ready to go forward as soon as you get the green light from God. It is neither wise to do the wrong thing nor to do nothing; instead, be diligent with what you have at hand.

The scripture reminds us in Proverbs 12:24 *that the hand of the diligent shall bear rule, but the slothful shall be under tribute.*

In other words, there is no shortcut to the top - let no one deceive you.

Diligence comes with perseverance and commitment, which most teenagers are unprepared to champion.

Dear reader, you are on the path to being diligent, as it takes commitment to pick a book to want to read. You must understand and be thoughtful about this: a diligent teenager has an edge over one who is not because hours dedicated towards realizing a goal eventually become the deciding factor for their extraordinary success in life.

Anything is achievable if you set your heart to it!

Chapter 2

VALUE YOUR TEENHOOD...

Let no man despise your youth, but you be an example to them that believe, in word, in manner of life, in love, in faith, in purity. (1 Tim 4:12)

The Scriptures describe the youthful age as a time of danger and challenge. Moses said that the imagination of a man's heart is evil from his youth (Gen 8:21) and Paul admonished Timothy to flee youthful lusts (2 Tim 2:22). On the other hand, God recognises the value of the youth for a divine cause. As a teenager you are energetic and daring; your hearts are filled with visions of the future. Indeed, you are the most valuable component in the service of God.

If all you think about your teen phase is that it is a frustrating time in life, you can't value your teenage years. If your only feeling is that it is the period when you're barely old enough to be on your own, or struggling to find some sense of identity, you can't enjoy it.

Isn't that why you sometimes try to act out, dress weirdly, or prove to be someone else?

Trying to act older than your age sometimes isn't a bad thing, but if you don't cherish and value your years now, you will not be living fully in the moment. Wishing to be older is a funny thing - many people trade their teenage years for peer pressure, fame, and fake lifestyles. Wishing to be older, richer, or someone else than who they really are causes them to stop living.

The simple truth is that we do not value our years if all we do is wish we had more. Stop dreaming of the future, turn your dream into your future instead. You don't have to be timid. You have nothing to fear.

Fear ye not, therefore, ye are of more value than many sparrows. Matt 10:31

Solomon, who wasted his youth in total exuberance, thought better of the matter in his declining days and asserted, *remember now your creator in the days of your youth, before the evil days come and the years draw near when you will say, I have no pleasure in them (Ecclesiastics 12:1).* Now that you are still a teenager, you must understand that your value is inestimable, and the resources embedded in you to be great must not be traded for any form of vice or negligence. When you recognise your value then you can accomplish magnificent things for the glory of God

Do you understand why you do what you do? Have you ever given thought to this? What guides your choice? How do you make decisions that you carry out eventually? Are you doing what you are meant to do? Do you know that God is more concerned about why you do things rather than what you do? Remember that the scripture admonishes us that all works done from a wrong motive will be destroyed (1 Corin 3:3–15).

Only those who value themselves can give meaningful reasons for the things they engage in. It is possible to know your life purpose and spend your life doing it but with the wrong motive in your heart. For example, you know God has called you to study medicine, but you are pursuing that career seeking to find your worth in it (to feel important, admired, and well thought of) when you should rather find it in being God's child and knowing who you are in Christ. The truth is that you may not be happy in that career because you have not found your place in what Christ has planned for you in that career for his glory.

In all these, you must understand that understanding your personality is key in teenagehood. It's a time when you begin to explore and assert your personal identities. During this period, you engage in a search for where you fit in with your peers and society at large. It is common for you to have an unstable sense of self and try out new personal labels and associate with various peer groups. Additionally, you might struggle to define your sexual and gender identity during your teenage years. Through whatever challenges you experience during this transition stage, hold high your values and work towards establishing a Christlike personality.

Your values

What you count as important in the way you live every day will determine your priorities and also measure the decisions you make in life. The people around you have values that influence you. That's just the way the world works. Your parents have values. Your faith community has values. Your neighbourhood and nation have values. Your school has values. Teams that you are on or organisations that you belong to have values. These values may be similar to yours, or there may be a good deal of conflict between them. They may be forcefully presented to you, or may simply exist in your world and exert less direct influence.

The pitfall is in simply accepting these values without asking if they are right for you. Many of them will be right for you. Some will not be right for you, and it can be intimidating to adopt values that are different from those around you, which is why you must understand what your values are.

When the things that you do and the way you behave match your values, life is usually good. You are satisfied and content. But when these don't align with your personal values, that's when things feel... wrong. This can become a real source of unhappiness.

Making a conscious effort to identify your values is so important.

How Values Help You

Values exist, whether you recognize them or not. Life is much easier when you acknowledge your values and make plans and decisions that honour them. Let me explain: if you value education but you spend most of your spare time playing, you will not feel fulfilled. If you value God and your relationship with Him, you want to put Him first; but if you find yourself with others who don't value the things of God, their values may override yours and you are likely to be shaped by their values.

In these types of situations, understanding your values can help. When you know your own values, you can use them to make decisions about how to live your life. When you define your personal values, you discover what's truly important to you.

A good way to start doing this is to look back on your life and identify when you felt really good and confident that you were making good choices.

To own your values actually is a good way to start paying close attention to what inspires you and looking back to the things you need to change or recreate and also identify those actions, thoughts that makes you feel good, confident in other to make the right choices going forward.

Chapter 3

GOD PROMISE FOR YOU

"For I know the plans I have for you," declares the Lord, plans to prosper you and not to harm you, plans to give you hope and a future (Jer 29:11).

When you are wise enough to know that someone has a great plan for you, what do you do? Do you ignore the person or embrace him? I know you are wise enough to embrace that person in order to unfold the plan and purpose for your life. God is practically saying *"I know the plan I have for you, a plan that is good not evil."* Why can't you be patient to know Him so that He can unfold this plan to you regularly? The world or the devil equally has a plan for you, but believe me, it is not a good one. It is to distract, entice, and deceive you so that the good plan of God will not stand.

19

Say God forbid with all your breath.

Hear what Isaiah 30:1 says, *Ah, stubborn children, declares the Lord, who carry out a plan but not mine and who make an alliance but not of my spirit that they may add sin to sin.*

You see, stubbornness is rebellion against God's plan and purpose. Before God formed you in the womb, He knew you. Before you were born, He set you apart for greatness (Jeremiah 1:5). The architect of your life has the plan, allow Him to design you unto greatness. Stop looking for a plan that will never work for you, it is going to be a waste of time.

God's plan for you is to prosper you. Do you know what this means?

Chapter 4

CONTENDERS OF YOUR PROMISE

"For I know the thoughts that I think towards you," saith the Lord, "thoughts of peace and not of evil, to give you an expected end." (Jeremiah 29:11)

This statement is God's promise for you that should flood your mind; unfortunately, because it is not something you can see or lay hold on now, you exert your energy on things that will not make you walk in this promise. The enemy takes advantage of your non-acknowledgement of God's promises by introducing things that will keep you drifting away from his promises; these things I have referred to as contenders of your promise.

You and I know very well that a promise is a promise once stated, except if one of the parties involved refuses to act upon it, or the recipient forgets about the promise and treats it as not relevant. When we are careless with the promises of God, they can be truncated. In essence, one of the biggest contenders of God's promises in our life is ***forgetfulness***. The Lord will enlighten your understanding of this truth as it is not perceived as something that could delay God's promise upon your life. Hosea 4:6 says *my people are destroyed for lack of knowledge: because thou have rejected knowledge, I will also reject thee, that thou shalt be no priest to me; seeing thou hast forgotten the law of thy God, I will also forget thy children.*

God is telling you what can destroy you and it still does not ring a bell to you that God's word is knowledge and the knowledge of Him is your power to destroy every form of evil contending against the reality of God's promises upon you. Many times, when these promises are delivered, we are supposed to engage them, but we rather drop them at God's lap, expecting Him to do everything in His sovereignty.

Let's take a cue from Daniel. All through his life, Daniel studied the scriptures that had gone before him and hoped diligently for their fulfilment. He understood the plans of God, so, he ensured that he did not love the pleasures of life (Daniel 9:1–3). He set his face to seek the Lord by prayer and supplication.

As a teenager, you hear God's word as you read by yourself, hear it from the altar, or hear it on social media every time. Have you ever sought further to know how it will be fulfilled in your life? I guess I would not be wrong if I said you rejoiced as you received the words of promise but forgot about them after a while—you stopped giving attention to them. May forgetfulness not contend against God's promise upon your life in Jesus' name.

You cannot find expression as a teenager until you lay hold on God's promises, that is, until you know His mind concerning you.

Another major contender against God's promise upon you is your *time*. Ecclesiastics 3:1 tells us that *to everything there is a season and a time to every purpose under heaven*. Your season as a teenager is for a purpose that must be fulfilled. Your purpose for every season comes with God's promise, and time is a great determiner for it to come to pass in your life. My point is this: the amount of light that will radiate in your life is dependent on the amount of time you give to what God has for you.

24

The things you spend more time doing rub off on you. Create time to study God's word, pray those words, and sing those words.

It will become easy to want more of the things of God.

Chapter 5

LITTLE FOXES

Take us the foxes, the little foxes that spoil the vine, for our vines have tender grapes. Songs of Solomon 2:15

Give your eyes no sleep, and your eyelids no slumber... Go to the ant, O sluggard; consider her ways and be wise. Prov. 6:4-6

What are the little foxes causing you to not achieve your purpose in life or those enviable dreams? This fascinating story in Solomon's song contains many intriguing pictures. One is of a beautiful vineyard in early spring; the vines, however, are threatened by little foxes that come in to eat the tender grapes before they are ripe. Solomon calls our attention to these seemingly insignificant little foxes that come in every day to spoil the vine. This is a warning to you and me about the little things in life that bring us down. Those seemingly insignificant things cause grossly disproportionate damage. We must therefore guard ourselves against little foxes that bring harm to our lives.

Little foxes could reflect in our lives as our attitude, laziness, tongue, and ingratitude.

Yet a little sleep, a little slumber, a little folding of the hands to sleep; so, shall thy poverty come as one that travailed, and thy want as an armed man. Prov.6:10

Laziness spoils the vine of birthing industries and success. Ultimately, the lazy person will come to poverty. So, wake up! Get out of bed, out of your place of comfort, and get busy before it is too late. Sleep is sweet, but continual sleep leads to poverty and sluggishness, like the sloth, who would sleep all day if it had its way. Chase the little fox of laziness from your vineyard, or you'll have no vine, no grapes, and no profit.

Even so, the tongue is a little member and boasts great things. Behold, how great a matter a little fire kindled! James 3:5

Blasphemy, lying, gossiping, cursing, and backbiting are all associated with the tongue, amongst others. Words hurt, don't they? A little spewing of the tongue can do irreparable damage to a life, so, bite your tongue before it bites you. Let the words of your mouth be edifying and acceptable to God. As teenagers, our tongue has a lot of power. Proverbs 18:21 confirms this by saying, "*Death and life are in the power of the tongue, and those who love it will eat its fruit.*"

Tell yourself boldly, "I will eat the fruit of life in Jesus' name."

> *For who hath despised the day of small things? Zec. 4:10*

To the wise, little things count.

The Lord resents ingratitude. *In everything give thanks; for this is the will of God in Christ Jesus concerning you (Rom 1:21; 1 Thessalonians 5:18).*

Have you ever done something for someone and never received so much as a thank you? It hurt, didn't it?

Do you know that it hurts the Lord when we are given so much every day but don't thank him?

Thus, as teenagers, you must be grateful for the moment and stage you are in now. You can only enjoy what you have experienced, not what you are yet to experience. So, enjoy the moment as a teenager and give thanks to God as He prepares you for the next stage.

You must fight whichever little thing portrays itself as the little fox in your life with all wisdom and understanding before it destroys you. Wisdom is profitable to direct in all our ways; consider the wisdom of the ant. Those who despise the importance of little things are in danger of becoming little people; no great man will ever do so. He will rather prove his greatness by a hearty recognition of the truth of the wise saying, "He who despises little things shall fall little by little."

Whenever I found it difficult to start or do something new, my dad would always tell me that little drops of water make a mighty ocean. I only need to put in a little consistent effort, and it has always helped me. Remember the Syrian warrior who refused to wash in the river Jordan according to the prophet's direction because he could not see how something so little could affect his cure; but when persuaded to do it by a wise and faithful servant, he found that, as minute as the instruction sounds, it wrought his salvation.

I trust God to help you make the right choice and to be wise.

Chapter 6

THE POWER OF YOUR CHOICE

See, I have set before thee this day life and good, and death and evil. (Deuteronomy 30:15)

We all have a will and a choice, and if something doesn't go our way or we don't like where we stand, we can change that. Decision-making is oftentimes not as challenging as it sounds. We make daily decisions without putting much thought into them, from waking up in the morning to going to bed. The choices we make every day are part of our routine, so less thought goes into them. However, the circumstances or the people associated with choices can make it hard because relationships and emotions are involved. Sometimes the choices we make can be life-changing; they determine who we are as a person and can leave us with more meaningful learning experiences.

Life isn't a bed of roses. There will be moments in your life when decision-making is resilient. Often, the thought of the unknown and what lies subsequently in our lives sends chills down our spine because we cannot see it. Life is all about choices. Every second, we make a choice. Either we are choosing to do something or not do something. Our choices shape our lives. Such is the power of choice.

Come to think of it, our lives are nothing but an aggregate of all the choices we have made so far, isn't it?

Every choice we make places a door in front of us that opens an unfolding pathway. As a young teenager, you have so many options open to you, and you are wondering: what do I do? Where should I go? Who should I tell? All these things going through your head can be quite a fright if not well considered. But whether you like it or not, whatever choice you make at any point will either make you or destroy you.

That brings us to what kind of choice you are actually making at every point in your life. How relevant is it to your life? Have you sought God in prayers regarding it? Have you shared it with your parents or someone you trust? All these are processes that help guide you in making the right choices in life. Never be afraid to tell or share, even when you know it will not be approved or heard. Your choices are still dependent on your parent's approval, so why hide from them? If you hide anything from your parents, then be ready for the consequences. Be bold and humble enough to tell if it is sincere, but remember the words of Joshua, "Choose you this day whom you will serve...But as for me and my house, we will serve the Lord." (Joshua 24:15)

The thing that sets all mortals apart is the ability to make choices. Most importantly, we have the power to choose the relationships we develop with people.

I keep asking myself, why the opportunity to make choices? God has given us the choice of life and death. You know, when God made man, He made man in His own image and likeness, and one of the characteristics of God's nature is His self-determination. Being in His image means we were also created as self-determining beings. That means I have and can exercise my will to choose to do good or evil. Creating man without the capacity for choice would be meaningless if there weren't something to choose.

Do you now see why we have a lot of things that are attractive and desirable? Your choice of capacity needs to be exercised appropriately. In other words, we actually become the product of our choices. You really can't blame God for what you have become; you are what you are as a result of the choices you have made. Opportunities don't just fall out of the sky into your laps, you create them, you hunt them, you discover them, and it all happens based on the kind of choice you make. Stop trying to do something big all the time, rather, focus on the thousands of small choices that you make on an everyday basis because ultimately they are going to be the deciding factor in your life.

The path of choosing evil begins when you allow your heart to turn away from God. Then you find yourself refusing to hear from God by not reading the Bible, neglecting parental instruction, and making excuses for your actions. Then you begin to neglect coming to church, you refuse to heed the warnings of the Spirit in your heart. You find yourself drawn away and you begin to worship other gods—the god of sensual pleasure.

Watch it: when your love for sport begins to exceed your love for God, you begin to worship the creation, more than the creator, you worship success. The reward is death because the wages of sin is death; you will now be exposed to the evil that Satan desires to bring into your life. This shall not be your story if your choice is to choose life. I know this looks as though it's tough to achieve considering the environment and society we find ourselves in today. That is why the scriptures assure us in Isaiah 41:10: *fear thou not, for I am with you; be not dismayed for I am thy God; I will strengthen you, yes, I will help you, and hold you with the right hand of my righteousness.*

That's a sure word, which I have held on to strongly till today. Of course, there is a reward for those who make good choices.

Chapter 7

YOUR REWARD

God will repay each person according to what they have done.
Romans 2:6

As a teenager, what is your reward?

Our lives are filled with many choices on how to spend our time, energy, and resources; what to expect in the future; and especially what we want to become as teens. Everything we think, say and do has consequences for ourselves and others. Like ripples on a pond, our actions spread out and affect others because everything is interconnected. While we are free to choose our actions, we are not free to choose the consequences of our actions. This is one of the main reasons I chose to write this book. Your teenage years are precious, and you must treasure them; they must not slip away from you carelessly.

34

Learn to value your youth, understand who you are, and know God's promise for you. This visualisation will make you remember that for everything you do, there is a reward, whether good or bad. The reward of what you invest your time in now will speak for you gallantly before you know it.

What are these likely rewards?

1. Reward of peace

Anxiety in teenagers or adolescents is a common feeling. However, when it begins to disrupt your everyday activities and create tension and stress, it needs to be examined more seriously. An anxious teenager experiences low concentration, physical aches and pain, as well as low confidence and self-esteem. The book of Philippians 4:6-7 says *do not be anxious about anything, but in every situation, by prayer and petition, with thanksgiving, present your requests to God. And the **peace of God**, which transcends all understanding, will guard your hearts and your minds in Christ Jesus.*

The reward of peace comes at a cost of praying and creating a good relationship with God. Then your heart and mind will be guarded against all manner of anxiety and fear of the unknown.

2. Reward of salvation

A long time ago, God has had things He planned for you to do. Are you going to complain about how impossible the task seems to you or are you going to step out in faith and trust that when you partner with God, He can do so much more in and through you than you have ever imagined? Proverbs 3:5-6 says *Trust in the LORD with all your heart and lean not on your own understanding; in all your ways submit to him, and he will make your paths straight.*

With your total reliance and submission to God comes the reward of salvation. Your straight path is your gateway to life.

Psalm 149:4 says the Lord will beautify the meek with His salvation.

3. Reward of rest

Have you ever had a time in your life when you felt overwhelmed by the things of this world? Where life seemed so hard and no matter what you did, things just wouldn't go right? In my life, I have come to realise that whenever I try to do everything with my own strength alone (without the help of God), it does not always turn out well.

36

When you are heavy-laden it is as if your spirit, mind, will, and emotions can't function because there is this weight on you that you try to lift by yourself. It causes you to feel sad, depressed, anxious, and all those negative emotions that you do not want in life. Here is the good news: Matthew 11:28-30 says,

"Come to me, all you who are weary and burdened, and I will give you rest. Take my yoke upon you and learn from me, for I am gentle and humble in heart, and you will find rest for your souls. For my yoke is easy and my burden is light." Come to the Lord and watch Him give you rest from fear, hopelessness, addiction, and all sort of depression.

4. The reward of fruitfulness in due season

Every good tree produces its fruit in due season. Only good seeds produce good fruit. Your season of sowing as a teenager is now. Sow seeds of righteousness amid thorns.

Galatians 6:9 says *Let us not become weary in doing good, for at the proper time we will reap a harvest if we do not give up.*

In the process of understanding who you are, always know that every decision you take now is a seed, and there will be a reward for each.

5.Reward of longevity

God's word in Exodus 20:12 says *Honour your father and your mother, so that you may live long in the land the LORD your God is giving you.* When you honour your parents by simply obeying, I assure you that you will naturally enjoy peace and experience calmness, becoming more responsible and emphatic. These are pointers to your longevity.

A teenager that is always disobedient, and disrespectful can't enjoy peace because you can't be trusted to do things ordinarily that you are capable of doing, which of course could make you feel less confident, impulsive, fearful, rude and much more, truncating your joy.

Your reward of longevity lies in your joy. It is solely dependent on how much personal commitment, and effort you have put into something good without necessarily being told all the time. Your future as a teenager is greatly dependent on these rewards.

Finally, dear teen, honour, blessing, and recompense in heaven are not promised simply as payment for injustices suffered in this life but specifically for "those who pay the price to live a righteous life" (Matthew 5:10). God has a special prize set aside for believers who are insulted, mocked, punished, and treated unfairly because of their stand and testimony for Jesus Christ. These are Christians who eagerly practice kingdom righteousness and suffer for it.

As a teenager would you be bold enough to be mocked because you talked to someone about Jesus in your school or be bold to say no to drugs, fornication, stealing because you know the Lord? This is an acid test for you any day.

Only resilient teenagers can turn challenges into triumphs and live to see the good of the next days.

Chapter 8

FOR A BRIGHTER FUTURE

Be careful for nothing, but in everything by prayer and supplication with thanksgiving let your request be made known unto God (Philippians 4:6).

One thing however remains true about many young teenagers: they are optimistic but anxious about their future already. Anxiety is a tricky thing, isn't it? Yet, God commands us not to be anxious (Philippians 4:4-6).

In reality, you can't help but feel bodily reactions to seemingly fearful situations. It is part of what makes you human. The one thing that has helped me the most is growing in my understanding of

God's providential care for me. If He takes care of the birds, He'll also take care of you and your future. When your future arrives, what you need to know is that God will be right there with you, and that is more than enough. Allow the Lord to shape your character as you look to him in this season because your future is no doubt bright.

The only perfect plan is God's.

If you could see your life in 50 years, then you wouldn't need God- you'd be in control of your own life, but I tell you you'd mess it up pretty badly even then. This is why you need God. Sometimes, you find yourself waiting for that perfect light bulb moment where you figure out your future even though you know you should just trust God. If you stay on His path and obey Him, you'll know what you need to know when you need to know it because God has your future figured out already.

But it is just so hard to simply…wait, isn't it?

Waiting for the future.

What are you supposed to do while you are waiting for everything to finally make sense?

Simple.

Stay in God's path.

I'm not ready to know my future because right now, I'm dependent on myself. I'm not waiting patiently.

Maybe you're not either; I understand.

It's hard to watch your friends excitedly discuss their plans when you are clueless. They seem to have it all figured out (well, you might assume so but it's not always the case). It's okay to get excited when you finish high school, get admission to the university, get a new job, serve in the church, or try new skills and hobbies. Celebrate as you walk through this season of life because it's a gift. Even when you know things are playing out tough, bear in mind that your life doesn't start when you enter college, get a job, or get married. Your life doesn't start when you figure out what to do with your life. Your life doesn't start when the lightbulb comes on.

Your life is already begun even before you realise you are a teenager!

God knows best.

Even if God revealed his step-by-step plan for your life right now, I'm not sure you would be ready for it!

If God told me then I would be in Kwara with my family, I'd be far from ready right now. I'd probably be kicking and screaming against it in my mind because that place never crossed my thought as a teenager. Invariably, you need to wait patiently, knowing that He will guide you on your path at the right time.

As Christian teenagers, we don't have to trust ourselves to come up with the best plan for the future, and I trust that should be a relief! *"So do not worry about tomorrow; for tomorrow will care for itself. Each day has enough trouble of its own"* (Matthew 6:34). *"And which of you by worrying can add a single hour to his life's span?"* (Luke 12:25).

"For I know the plans that I have for you,' declares the Lord, 'plans for good and not for calamity to give you a future and a hope. Then you will call upon Me and come and pray to Me, and I will listen to

you. You will seek Me and find Me when you search for Me with all your heart" (Jeremiah 29:11-13).

We're not supposed to worry about tomorrow because it makes us miserable. Trusting God brings peace. He promised that if we try to grow close to Him, He will let us find Him.

Remember this the next time you're worried about the future:

1. God's plan and timing are perfect. You may doubt them at times, but that doesn't mean He doesn't love you and have the right life planned for you.

    When you're supposed to know His will, you'll know.

2. When you're sitting up all night thinking about the path ahead, stop looking inward and start looking upward to God.

    Pray and ask for His help.

3. Maybe you're not ready to know the future yet. Sometimes knowing the future can be scarier than not knowing.

4. You aren't the only one who is unsure of God's will. There are many others just like you and I, but your assurance is this that *the path of the just is as the shining light, that shineth more*

and more unto the perfect day (Proverbs 4:18)

5.   You can do other things while you wait. This is the time to try new things and figure out what you enjoy. The time to reflect on the kind of person God wants you to be before you figure out what He wants you to do and how.

The steps of a man are established by the Lord, when he delights in his way even when you stumble at times, you will not fall because He will uphold you with his hand. Psalm (37: 23-24)

Don't rely on your planner; don't rely on yourself to create a good future. It won't be nearly as wonderful as the one God has planned for you. Rather, crave for the things of God- what this means is that whatsoever plan you make, whatsoever desire you have, commit it to God and ask for His guidance on every step to take.

Let God be the centre of every decision you make, and I can assure you that you cannot go wrong!

Chapter 9

CRAVING FOR IT

Flee from youthful passions and crave for righteousness, faith love and peace. 2 Tim 2:22

Every teenager craves different things at different times, but let me shock you.

Do you know that most teenagers crave the same things? Not new clothes, shoes, gadgets, sex, freedom, cars or even money but **praise.** The craving to be praised and recognised makes them want a new dress, shoe or something.

As Christian teenagers, Paul warns us against short-sighted cravings of youth for personal pleasures or gain, rather than for personal godliness.

Youthful cravings or lust could be a kind of hunger or ambition that distracts one from his or her pursuit of true righteousness and peace.

A craving is a powerful desire for something experienced by all humans. As a teenager, you are not wrong if you have a craving, but the question is what kind of things do you crave? Are they fulfilling? Or mere chasing of the shadows? In this context, a craving is captured as a desire for God that enables you to flee youthful lust.

Remember the beatitude of Jesus in Matthew 5:6 which says, *"Blessed are those who hunger and thirst for righteousness, for they shall be satisfied."* To hunger and thirst for righteousness is a state of being. It isn't a once-and-done ordeal but an indefinite desire and pursuit. Like an appetite, even though once satisfied, still burns, and must be regularly sought after. On the other hand, someone without a hunger and thirst for righteousness isn't seeking God. They tend not to have any desire for Him, no need to even search, no awareness, and thus may never find Him. These are those that are spiritually dead and ignorantly indifferent to what they lack.

Today, I encourage you to be sensitive enough to know whether your hunger for righteousness is alive and if yes keep the flame burning.

Timothy was a young man. Paul knew the danger of young men being overcome by youthful lusts, therefore exhorts Timothy to "Flee also youthful lusts." I, in much earnestness of heart, likewise exhort you, young reader, to flee away from youthful lusts. Keep away from those things that have any power to lure you away from God and spiritual exercise. We could tell you of scores of boys and girls, who were once blessedly saved, but who have gone back into the ways of sin, all because they did not keep aloof from those things that tempt to mind fleshly things.

Many young Christians have gone down in defeat because of too much association with young people who are living sinful lives. Most times you struggle with deciding how you associate with them because of a reason that is not justifiable. This does not mean that we cannot go among them at all, but it does mean that we are to be guarded and never to come down out of our sacred spiritual realm and strike a line of fellowship or affiliation with them. You should go among them as God leads so that you might win them to Christ. But you will need to keep yourself surrounded by a heavenly atmosphere that no spirit of worldliness can penetrate.
You are to lift them up. Beware, lest they drag you down.

God has made us social creatures to associate together. But young and old should be careful of the spirit of associations. Christian teenagers can associate together and lose spirituality by the manner or spirit in which they have been associated. They can also associate together in such a manner as to be greatly benefitted in a spiritual way by the association. Yet, it is very easy for young people to gain a greater love for the association with one another than for communion with God. The religious meetings of young people can very easily become a mere social gathering rather than a religious spiritual service. If they are a little watchful, they can determine which they enjoy most, the service itself, or the chatting together after the religious service is dismissed.

You must be intentional about every association and the reason for the association so you do not get carried away!

Chapter 10

SHARED THOUGHT

"Something horrible happened to me in January that made me want to finally commit myself to Christ and just genuinely become closer to Him. I started so well, read my Bible regularly and even started slowly giving up the worldly things that caused me to sin or to deviate from my path. I won't lie, to fully commit yourself to Christ is really hard at first because of the number of things you have to give up on that you are already used to doing.

Along the line I started slowly going back to my old habits, slacking when it comes to reading my Bible and just going back to the old ways slowly. I feel like the people around me distract me and make me do some things that I know deep inside I wouldn't want to do. In fact, I feel ashamed to even ask God for forgiveness because I promised Him I will change but I ended up not changing.

What is your advice for me? I want to be able to cut all distractions and begin my spiritual journey again with a fresh start."

This was from a teenager who needed advice on how to get on connected back to God. This can be you at some point in time of your life or maybe you might as well know a friend who is going through this. The first thing to understand about the shared thought is that the teenager realised he needed to align himself with God his father. This realisation was brave because it is the baby step needed for God to say "It's okay, don't be afraid, you don't have to be worried. I am with you to help you through this journey."

The teenager's mind is being shared and the genuine intention to return to the right path is created. However, I want you to know that your genuine intention most times comes with a struggle that you must constantly fight in other to be victorious.

My advice comes from the place of fatherly love. Remember 1 John 3:1 *How great is the love the Father has lavished on us! That we should be called children of God.* Every teenager wants to make his father proud, and anytime he falls short of doing so, he feels ashamed and wants to withdraw for fear of being scolded.

Your father remains your father and the reason he needs to scold you is to correct you to stay in line towards your life path. The shame or guilt will go away if you are ready to listen to your father's correction and gradually disconnect from the things that distract you. You must also understand that it is a process you must experience to become who God wants you to be. So, abide with the Father and the thought of and a lifestyle of habitual sin is gradually washed away.

Everything that becomes your reality stems from your thought…. Be a thoughtful teenager.

Prayer

Reading through this book I know would have taught you something unique to what you already know. This also mean that taking time to read spells out how special you are in wanting to add value to your life. To this point my prayer for you is that;

God almighty will lift you up above your widest imagination and order your steps as you make life changing decisions. I pray that the lord will steer you towards the choice that will lead you closer to God and the one that will bring fruit to the kingdom and true joy to you. Every step in life will continuously scale you to new levels of achievement bringing glory to God. The lord bless you and keep from every harm in Jesus name.

Say Amen and so it is

Ekhoriyayi Lilian Arigidi is the Executive Director of a co-educational school in Ilorin,Educator, andMentor for Teenagers and Teachers hold an M.Ed. and PhD. in Educational Management from the University of Ilorin and the University of Ibadan respectively. She has been involved in teaching and training of educators and teenagers. She speaks at conferences and is passionate about collaborative learning and encouraging students from her experience. She is blessed with children.